EARTH'S BIOMES

GRASSLAND

EARTH'S BIOMES

GRASSLAND

TOM WARHOL

 Marshall Cavendish
Benchmark
New York

HIGHWOOD PUBLIC LIBRARY
102 Highwood Avenue
Highwood, IL 60040-1597
Phone: 847-432-5404

To the next Warhol generations—Richard, Drew, Jason, Ben, Alyssa, Katie, Emily, Matt, Dan (the man), Raven, Devin, Seth, Casey, and Ashley. We're leaving this rich world to you. Take good care of it.

Marshall Cavendish Benchmark
99 White Plains Road
Tarrytown, New York 10591-9001
www.marshallcavendish.us

Editor: Karen Ang
Editorial Director: Michelle Bisson
Art Director: Anahid Hamparian
Series Designer: Patrice Sheridan

Library of Congress Cataloging-in-Publication Data

Warhol, Tom.
Grassland / by Tom Warhol.
p. cm.—(Earth's biomes)
Summary: "Explores grassland biomes and covers where they are located as well as the plants and animals that inhabit them"—Provided by publisher.
Includes bibliographical references and index.
ISBN-13: 978-0-7614-2196-2
ISBN-10: 0-7614-2196-3
1. Grassland ecology—Juvenile literature. 2. Grasslands—Juvenile literature. I. Title. II. Series.

QH541.5.P7W27 2007
577.4—dc22
2006015820

Front cover: A lion prowling through African grassland
Title page: A greater rhea
Back cover: Pronghorn

Photo research by Candlepants, Inc.

Cover Photo: Photononstop/ Super Stock

The photographs in this book are used by permission and through the courtesy of: *Minden Pictures:* Jim Brandenburg, 7, 16, 42, 54, 56; Carr Clifton, 8; Reg Morrison/Auscape, 14; Mitsuaki Iwago, 27; Martin Withers/FLPA, 28; Tim Fitzharris, 31; Frans Lanting, 35, 3, 63, 71; Goetz Eichhorn/Foto Natura, 43; Tui De Roy, 52, 67; Pete Oxford, 58, 66. *Photo Researchers Inc.:* Dr. Jeremy Burgess, 19; Dan Suzio, 20; James Steinberg, 22, 49; Alan & Linda Detrick, 25; James P. Jackson, 30; Jacana, 32; Jacques Jangoux, 33; Dennis Flaherty, 36; Bill Bachmann, 39; Tom McHugh, 46; James Zipp, 50; Thomas & Pat Leeson, 55, 68, back cover; Mark Boulton, 60; Francois Gohier, 65; David R. Frazier, 73. *Tom Warhol:* 40, 74, 62.

Printed in China
1 3 5 6 4 2

CONTENTS

INTRODUCTION

GRASSLANDS, THEN AND NOW

The chittering call sounds across the open North American shortgrass prairie, causing all the prairie dogs of the colony within earshot to cease their foraging and stand up tall and still. The smell of smoke and the crackle of the oncoming flames as they burn the dry grass are now easily detected by all. The squirrel-like rodents scramble for the nearest entrance to their underground maze of burrows.

Lightning strikes, common with the many storms that rage through grasslands, easily ignite the grasses and herbs, which have been dried for weeks by the relentless heat. Smoke billows from the ground and rises into the sky in columns, then it slants windward and collects into a great white mass. The smoke replaces the dense clouds that have blown away with the lightning storm that ignited the fire.

Just the day before, these tall grasses had swayed in the hot, dry summer breeze. But the grasses are now divided—the plants' liquids transformed into the smoke rising skyward and the solid, carbon matter reduced to ashes that will soon become part of the soil.

The surface of the ground reaches a blistering temperature, hot enough to quickly kill any creatures foolish enough to remain aboveground. The lizards, insects, and small mammals that are able to outrun

The open sky and treeless expanses of grasslands, or prairies as they're known in the United States, create a dynamic landscape of wind, rain, and fire.

the blaze are picked off by the hawks that soar or perch in the scattered trees and shrubs dotting the landscape ahead of the advancing flames. Larger animals, such as grazing buffalo or pronghorn, can usually outrun the fires. They move on to other, unburned grasslands, feeding on the grasses and herbs.

Huddled in many cool caverns in the darkness, the prairie dog colony waits, safe and insulated in their underground refuge. The roar of the flames grows louder as the strong, steady winds push the flames on, while the grasses feed the fire's massive appetite.

After the fire passes and the ground begins to cool, the prairie dogs emerge from their burrows to see a blackened, smoky landscape. However, this is not the disaster it may seem. In a few short months— or even weeks if conditions are right—the grasses and herbs will sprout again. By the next growing season, there will be lush growth, and the buffalo and pronghorn will return.

The prairie dogs may also have to range farther to find food for a few months until the next growing season begins. But soon their burrows will once again be surrounded by the grasses and herbs they rely upon for survival.

These are the sights and sounds of the grassland being reborn.

In the Great Basin of Nevada, mountains rise like islands above the flat expanses of grassland. Here, fences divide grazing properties.

1

EVOLUTION OF GRASSLANDS

Climate plays a very important role in where grasslands evolve and grow. Temperature and rainfall in the right amounts and at the right times allow grasses to grow but prevent other plants from taking hold. The climate has changed over the hundreds of millions of years that Earth has been evolving with plant life. So too has the arrangement of ecosystems and biomes changed over the surface of the planet.

Grasses themselves only evolved about sixty-five million years ago, around the time of the sudden extinction of the dinosaurs. Forests were still the dominant biome in the interiors of many continents. Grasslands formed as the continents were reshaping themselves, their tectonic plates shifting, causing mountain ranges to rise up gradually along the edges of land masses. About seventy million years ago, central North America, where today's prairies grow, was an inland sea. Fossils of sea creatures can still be found in the soils and rocks.

As North America's Rocky Mountains began to rise, the central sea began to drain, and dust and soil were blown and washed eastward, filling the central basin. The steeply rising western mountain ranges formed a barrier, preventing moist ocean air from flowing over land.

The interiors of the continent became drier, depriving trees of much needed moisture. A similar scenario played out in northern South America, where the *llanos,* a form of savanna, lie along the Orinoco River, sandwiched between the Andes and the Guyana Highlands.

As the forests died, the drought-tolerant grasses were able to colonize these hot, dry plains. The climate shifted from cool to warm and back again, bringing glaciers and evergreen forests south and north over time. Eventually, the grassland biome dominated the planet. Some researchers estimate that these formations covered nearly 45 percent of Earth's land surface (compared with 25 percent today). In North America, the first extensive grasslands are thought to have covered the central basin by 35 million years ago.

Many changes have occurred since then, but the grasslands have persisted in one form or another, resulting in the formations we see today.

GRASSLAND REGIONS

Grasslands can be found in both temperate and tropical regions of the world, usually between forest and desert biomes. The topography, or landscape, of grasslands tends to be level to gently rolling terrain, perfect for grass growth as it allows a maximum amount of sun to reach the plants. Forest regions, by contrast, are usually found on steeper slopes, mountains, and along rivers and streams.

As the name suggests, the plant life of grasslands consists mostly of grasses. However, many herbs grow alongside the grasses and can even outnumber them in some cases. In some formations, such as savannas, shrubs and even trees can be common.

Temperate grasslands are found in the temperate climate zones, from 30 to 60 degrees latitude north and south. In North America, they are known as prairies or plains, and the largest expanses of them grow in the middle of the continent, in the Great Plains region of the United States.

In Europe and Asia, temperate grasslands are known as steppes and tend to be drier than other temperate forms. They grow in a long, narrow band that crosses the continent, from eastern Europe through western and central Asia, into northeast Asia.

Steppe-like grasslands known as *pampas* grow in the Patagonian region of Argentina and in neighboring Uruguay. Both Africa and Australia contain formations of this type, known as *velds* in South Africa and simply as grasslands in southern Australia.

Grasslands of the World

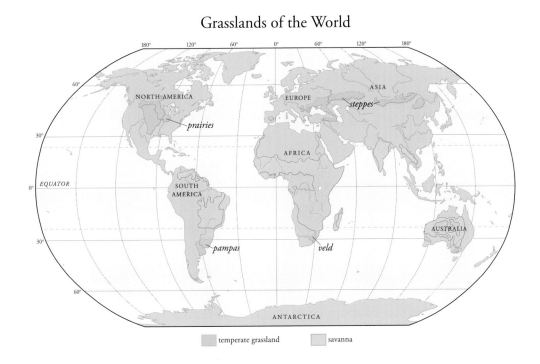

Tropical grasslands can be found mostly within 30 degrees latitude on either side of the equator. These grasslands are known as savannas, and the largest formation, the Serengeti Plain, is found in central and southern Africa. It supports an amazing variety of wildlife. Large areas of savanna also exist in Brazil, India, Southeast Asia, and Australia.

Unlike temperate grasslands, the grasses in savannas can grow among scattered smaller trees and shrubs. Types of savanna range from those made up exclusively of grasses and herbs to dry tropical forests. Savannas experience pronounced rainy and dry seasons, and fires occur regularly. Temperatures are high all year, but the heat can be particularly brutal during the dry season, with no moisture to relieve the heat.

Both plants and animals are diverse in tropical savannas. Grazing animals, such as buffalo, giraffes, wildebeests, zebras, gazelles, and antelopes, abound in the Serengeti. The variety of large herbivores—plant-eaters—provides a very good food source for the many species of carnivores—meat-eaters—such as cheetahs, lions, wild dogs, jackals, and hyenas.

MANAGED GRASSLANDS

Many grasslands in the world are artificial or semi-natural. They can be grown in nearly any climate. Pastures are grasslands that have been planted and used to house and feed (or graze) livestock, such as cattle, sheep, and goats. Rangelands, much larger managed grasslands, support a mix of natural grassland species and are used to graze livestock like cows and sheep.

Hayfields, another type of managed grassland, are usually made up of planted species. The grasses in these fields, or meadows, are harvested and used as feed for livestock. Nonnative plant species are prominent in all these types of managed grasslands.

With the human population increasing, and many suburban neighborhoods being built, a new form of grassland has been created. Small and large patches of single-species grass lawns have taken over much of the landscape in these areas. These nearly impenetrable mats of grass, artificially established, require a lot of care, water, fertilizers, and herbicides to maintain.

The natural cycles of the grass species used for lawns are completely altered to the point that the grasses grow constantly. Prevented— through regular mowing—from flowering and setting seed, lawns provide little in the way of habitat for any creature. Other plants that normally add essential nutrients to a naturally growing grassland are replaced by toxic chemicals that leach into the soil and the water supply. The United States alone has 30 million acres of lawn.

CLIMATE

Since grasslands exist in so many different locations on Earth, the temperature and rainfall patterns vary from formation to formation. While they don't occur in the driest or wettest areas of the globe (these are occupied by deserts and tropical forests, respectively), grasslands do grow in most climates in between.

The largest temperate grasslands occur in the middle of large continents, where the climate is relatively dry, winds are common, and temperatures fluctuate wildly between very cold and very hot both daily and throughout the year. There also may be extreme weather events, such as thunderstorms, snowstorms, tornadoes, dust storms, and droughts.

Savannas, which occur in tropical and subtropical areas, experience narrower temperature ranges than temperate grasslands. This means that they have less hot and less cold temperatures. There are also usually very marked rainy and dry seasons, with periods of drenching rains and long droughts.

Grasslands often experience specific rainy and dry seasons. This thunderstorm may bring relief or perhaps fire from lightning to the Northern Territory grasslands of Australia.

On the Serengeti Plain in central Africa, the rainy season begins in March with a *bang!* Thunderstorms bring heavy rains, one inch (2.5 centimeters) or more in a twenty-four-hour period. The savanna grasses grow quickly and vigorously in response, and animals give birth at this time, when the most food is available.

Intense storms signal the end of the rainy season as well, this time in October. The storms bring with them strong winds that dry out the plants. Between the winds and the constant, intense sun, by January the grasses are so dry that fires start easily from lightning strikes or matches.

SOILS, LIVING AND DEAD

One of the most important and defining characteristics of grasslands is the soil where the grasses grow. Soils vary with grassland type. The deep, dark soils of prairies support a diverse ecosystem. The top layers are dense with decaying organic material, called humus. The slow decomposition process releases nutrients at a rate and concentration that is ideal for prairie plants. The humus is light and airy, so it allows for good movement of water into the soil.

The densely packed roots of grassland plants hold the soil together, retaining water and providing a firm substrate for other plants to root in. The roots themselves, when they die, rot and return their nutrients to the soil.

Steppe soils are not as rich. They contain calcium carbonate salts left behind after water evaporates from the surface. These salts are toxic to many plants, so fewer species can grow here.

Savanna soils, particularly those of the Serengeti Plain in Africa and the llanos of South America, are also rich in salts. These salts become concentrated about 3 feet (1 meter) down into the soil and form what is known as a "hard pan." Tree roots are unable to penetrate this hard layer, which keeps any rainwater close to the surface, benefiting the grasses and herbs.

However, as with all other elements of this or any other biome or ecosystem, soil alone is not responsible for the fertility of grasslands. The climate plays an important role, and the grasses themselves add to and enrich the very soil they grow in and benefit from. In fact, savanna soils are so low in nutrients because as soon as dead plant matter decomposes, the many herbaceous savanna plants quickly absorb the nutrients that the plant matter has become.

While grasslands provide homes for many large plant-eaters, the most numerous animals that live in these habitats are insects, such as this twelve-spot skimmer dragonfly.

2

SEAS OF GRASSES

Weather, soils, and topography all play important roles in the makeup of grasslands, but it is the grass species themselves that are the real stars of this show. One of the most unusual groups in the plant kingdom, grasses provide habitat and food for an amazing array of other plants and animals, not the least of which are human beings.

With 300 families and 250,000 species, the angiosperms—the flowering plants—provide Earth with much of the basis for life. Grasses, wildflowers, and broad-leaved trees and shrubs are all angiosperms. Many species of animals and insects rely on plants for food, and many flowering plants rely on these same animals to help them reproduce. These relationships have existed for millions of years and hopefully will continue for many millions more.

The diversity of plants within the kingdom takes many forms, from small, delicate spring wildflowers like violets, to the world's largest single flower, the monstrous, fleshy, stinking *Rafflesia arnoldii* from Indonesia. Even among this wide diversity, grasses are unique.

GRASSES AND THEIR RELATIVES

With about 15,000 species, grasses and grasslike plants have evolved an amazing variety of forms. In the botanical world, the world of plants, only the orchid and aster families are larger than the grass family. There are about 10,000 species of true grasses, including the species most people are familiar with, those of lawns and gardens.

Grasses occur in more places in the world than any other flowering plants. Because they can grow so densely packed together, there are also many more individual grass plants in the world than there are members of any other plant family. They thrive under harsh conditions that many other plants cannot even tolerate, such as drought, extreme cold, strong winds, fire, and trampling by animals. Grasses can also regenerate new leaves after they've been cut. That is why they work so well for lawns.

Orchids and sunflowers have very showy and large flowers in order to attract insects or mammals, like bees and bats, to carry pollen from one flower to another so the plants can reproduce. In grasses and some other plants, however, wind carries pollen from one flower to another, so grasses don't need showy or aromatic flowers. Grasses are well adapted to life on open plains where the wind blows freely.

The grasslike plant families include the sedges, rushes, cattails, and arums. They have somewhat similar stem and leaf structures to the true grasses, but their flower structures differ.

GRASS ANATOMY

Grasses have the same basic structure as other flowering plants—stem, leaves, and flowers—but the parts are different enough to merit their own names. The single stem of a grass is known as the culm. It can be round or flat and made up of segments called joints. Where one joint meets another is called the node. The culms of most temperate-region grasses are hollow, except for the node. Tropical grasses have solid culms.

The leaves of some grasses grow only from the base of the culm, while many others have leaves growing from each node, branching alternately up the culm. Often the base of the leaf, known as the sheath, wraps around the node, protecting it, while the blade extends outward and upward as a long, pointed leaf.

The flowers of grasses grow at the top of the culm in differently shaped structures, known as spikes, heads, racemes, or panicles, depending upon the species. These structures are made up of many smaller segments called spikelets.

Open florets in the flower head of the common quackgrass, showing the anthers and stigmas—male and female reproductive parts.

Inside the spikelets are the florets, the part of the flower where fertilization takes place. Many thousands of spikelets can be produced by a single grass plant in only one season. When the florets are fertilized by pollen carried by the wind from another plant, an ovary inside the floret develops into a grain, or seed. These seeds are the parts of grasses that animals and humans eat. Wheat grains are ground into flour, and rice grains are cooked whole.

At just the right time, the spikelet breaks apart, allowing the grain to be carried away by the wind. When the grain lands on a bare patch of ground, it settles into the soil until conditions are right for it to germinate, or sprout, and it eventually develops into a mature grass.

Grasses also spread from their root systems and extensive underground stems. Culms of mat-forming grasses—species, such as buffalo

Culms arise and roots descend from the stolon of kikuyu grass, a mat-forming African grass which has become a weed in many grasslands of the world.

grass, that spread in an unbroken mat over large areas—grow from either a rhizome or a stolon. Rhizomes grow underground but are not roots. They are a type of stem, jointed like the culm, but growing horizontally, sending up new shoots called tillers from each node. Other mat grasses arise from a stolon, which is also a stem that grows horizontally, but, in this case, aboveground.

All of these structures are connected to a dense, miles-long system of fibrous roots that hold the soil together and are very efficient at absorbing moisture. In some species, such as big bluestem, the roots from a single grass plant may grow 6 feet (2 m) out from the plant and even farther down into the soil.

Grasses' ability to grow from their roots as well as sprouting from seed allows them to grow faster and take over areas more quickly than herbs or other plants.

HOW DO YOUR GRASSES GROW? BUNCHES AND MATS

The various grasslands of the world have certain characteristics based on the growth forms of the different grass species. Some grasses grow singly while others grow in groups.

Mat grasses, also known as sod or turf grasses, such as prairie cordgrass of North American prairies, grow mainly from rhizomes and stolons. These grasses cover large areas in mostly unbroken mats, growing so densely that they prevent other species of plants from taking root. Sod grasses are considered cool-season grasses because they grow most vigorously in spring and early summer, go dormant for the hot months of summer, then begin to grow again in the fall. They are native to cooler areas.

Kentucky bluegrass and ryegrass are turf grasses that are commonly used for lawns. European species that evolved over centuries of grazing by cattle and sheep, these grass species have adapted by growing low to the ground, away from the gnashing teeth of grazing livestock.

When left to continue their natural cycle, these plants turn brown in the heat of summer. They do this to prevent water loss and death. However, humans keep their lawns growing all summer by watering them constantly, an unwise use of water at a time when streams and rivers have little water to give.

As their name implies, bunchgrasses—such as little bluestem and blue grama—grow in clumps or bunches. They begin from a single plant and grow outward from the crown in a circle. Their deep roots make them survivors in areas prone to drought, like along the margins of deserts. The bunches also catch soil and even snow, which they can use for nutrients and moisture.

Bunchgrasses are considered warm-season grasses because they do most of their growing in the warmest parts of summer. They grow mainly in savannas, steppes, and warm prairies. Because they grow mostly in dry climates, bunchgrasses' growth and flowering are tied to the amount of moisture in the air.

Other plants growing amidst the blue grama and buffalo grass in Colorado transform the springtime landscape with their showy flowers.

Other plants can grow in the spaces between the scattered clumps, so bunch grasslands can be very diverse environments. Animals can move freely in bunchgrass ecosystems. Ground-nesting birds often make use of the spaces between bunches for their nests.

GRASSLAND PLANT ADAPTATIONS

Grasses are hardy plants, indeed. They are regularly dried out, burned, trampled, ripped up and chewed, planted in monocultures, and dug up once or twice a year. Grasses have come to be so diverse and to dominate the grassland biome because they have adapted to these harsh and changing conditions, enabling them to thrive when most plants would wither and die.

Many species of grasses store water in underground organs called bulbs and corms. These organs also contain growing points from which new tillers can be sent out, which will expand into new plants and leaves. The seeds of some grassland plants can lie dormant in the soil during dry periods. When enough rain falls and the temperatures are favorable, they will sprout.

Buffalo grass and blue grama are two shallow-rooted grass species that prevent water loss by curling their leaves to hold in the moisture. Fine, hairlike roots are efficient at soaking up small amounts of water from the soil.

While grazing can help encourage grass plants to grow, many grasses protect themselves from this pressure. Grasses grow from the base of the leaves outward, unlike other plants, which grow from the tips of leaves, branches, and stems. This allows grasses to continue to grow if they are clipped or eaten. The blades of many grass species are also ridged with fine, stiff hairs, making the leaves more difficult to chew and swallow.

In tropical savannas life may thrive during the relatively short rainy season, but staying alive during the dry season is particularly challenging. Many savanna plants have deep root systems to reach the reduced groundwater levels in times of drought.

Savanna trees also have deep roots to deal with drought, and some, like palms, have thick bark to protect them from the hot fires that rage in the dry season. The living part of most temperate tree trunks is in the outermost layer of wood, just below the bark. This can put them in danger when a hot fire burns. The living wood of palms is distributed throughout the trunk, so if fire burns through the tough bark, they can still survive. The inner wood will continue to carry water and sugars back and forth between the leaves and roots.

Just as some temperate woody plants lose their leaves in winter, some species of savanna woody plants lose their leaves in the dry season. In both cases, these plants are responding to a lack of water. In the temperate winter, the ground is often frozen, and water comes mostly as snow, little of which reaches the roots of plants. In savannas, the lack of rain in the dry season is the limiting growth factor.

BAMBOO

Bamboos are unique in the world of grasses. Part of the same family as the Poaceae, or true grasses, bamboos are either woody or herbaceous, and most are evergreen.

Herbaceous bamboos grow only in warm, moist tropical climates under forest shade. Most species grow from Mexico through South America and into Argentina, while only a few grow on other continents, like Asia and Africa.

The woody types are also known as tree grasses because they can grow as tall as trees. Not restricted to a specific climate or habitat, tree

Tree bamboos can grow very densely and tall. They are often grown in gardens, and the wood is used for building materials as well as furniture and toys.

bamboos occur on nearly every continent, but they grow best in tropical regions. Madagascar is very rich in tree bamboos, as are south and east Asia and tropical regions of North and South America.

Tree bamboos are very hearty, and they are considered the fastest growing woody plants on Earth. Some can grow as quickly as 12 inches (30 cm) a day. A few species have been known to grow as much as 39 inches (100 cm) in a single day! Woody bamboos can reach a height of 130 feet (40 m), and their stems can reach diameters of 12 inches (30 cm). Like trees but unlike most grasses, bamboos can have multiple side branches.

Bamboos are easily transplanted and are commonly grown in gardens. If left uncared for, they will quickly invade other areas. Their roots grow so deeply and spread out so widely that they are very difficult to remove. Scientists are unsure of exactly where bamboos first came from because they have been moved around the world and replanted so often.

More the king of the grassland than the king of the jungle, the African lion is the top predator of Africa's Serengeti Plain.

3

BEASTS AND FIRE

Grasslands are not important simply for the grasses and other plants that make up their vegetation. Other factors, such as animals and fire, help shape the grasslands. In fact, the grasslands would not exist in their present conditions without these influences. They are all integral parts of the biome.

GRASSLAND ECOLOGY

The many different animals that inhabit the various formations of the grassland biome around the world have, in many cases, evolved with their habitat, influencing it to the point that they are necessary to the proper functioning of the systems and processes that maintain the biome.

By focusing on their own preferred plant species, large grazing animals—such as bison, pronghorn, and bighorn sheep of the temperate grasslands, and antelopes, zebras, giraffes, wildebeests, gazelles, and

The European harvest mouse lives in grasslands and croplands from Europe through Mongolia. It grips the stems of tall grasses with its back legs and steadies itself with its tail, leaving its front feet free to gather seeds.

elephants of tropical savannas—help to keep these habitats stable. By eating certain grass species, they encourage those species to continue to grow.

These animals also help maintain the grassland in other ways. Their hooves kick the soil up, allowing plants to grow in new sites, and animal droppings return nutrients to the soil, feeding the plants.

Much more numerous than the grazing animals are the many rodents that live on and under the grasslands. Scientists estimate that 325,000 rodents can live in the same 4 square miles (10 square kilometers) of Eurasian steppe that can support only four saiga antelope. Whereas the saiga consume as much as 40 pounds (18 kilograms) of plants each day during the growing season, the rodents can eat more than two tons of grasses and other plants. In this way, rodents have a much larger impact on the steppe.

An open landscape like grassland holds many dangers for small rodents like mice, gophers, prairie dogs, and rabbits. They hide and escape from predators—meat-eating animals—by digging underground tunnels and caverns, called burrows. Grasslands are riddled with these underground networks.

The predators of the grasslands, such as hawks, snakes, wolves, coyotes, badgers, lions, cheetahs, leopards, and hyenas, help control the populations of the other two groups. Scavengers, such as jackals and vultures, clean up after the predators. Not a scrap of food is wasted.

Without these grassland hunters, the grazing and burrowing animal populations could possibly overwhelm their food source or damage the soil, reducing the amount of space for grasses to grow. However, if the populations of rodents drop—due to disease or drought, for example—the predators will suffer. A healthy ecosystem is one where the balance of predator and prey is maintained within a level of natural variation.

All the seeds that grassland plants produce are excellent food for birds. Many bird species breed—mate, give birth, and raise their young—in grasslands. Because there are few, if any, trees in grassland habitats, most birds have adapted by nesting on the ground and spending more time walking than flying. The Australian bustard, a large savanna bird, builds its nests in the dense grasses and runs from predators rather than flying away, though it is able to fly.

Grasslands also influence the behavior of some birds. Because there aren't a lot of good places to perch, many songbirds, such as bobolinks and larks, sing while they fly, to attract a mate or claim territory. Most forest-dwelling species do this from a perch.

SMALL IS BEAUTIFUL — AND POWERFUL

In terms of numbers of species and impact on the grassland community, the microscopic organisms that live in the soil may win out over others. Bacteria, fungi, and microfauna (small animals) perform the

Ruminant Digestion

Hand in hand—or, rather, hoof in hoof—with the evolution of grasslands was the evolution of hoofed mammals, such as the buffalo or the domesticated cow, that took advantage of the abundant, nutritious grasses.

However, grasses can be difficult for animals to digest. Some grazing animals have enzymes in their bodies to help them break down plant material, but ruminants, a group that includes cows, sheep, goats, deer, and giraffes, do not have this enzyme in their stomachs. In order to eat grasses, ruminants developed, over time, an entirely unique digestive system. These creatures have stomachs with four chambers.

A mouthful of grass pulled from the ground isn't chewed very much before being swallowed by a cow or a buffalo. Their stomachs do much of the early work. Bacteria in the first two stomachs soften the plants, then the softened wad of grasses is passed back up to the animals' mouths. The ruminant chews it and swallows it again, passing the wad back through the first two stomach chambers and on into the third and fourth, where the last of the nutrients are taken out, and the digestive process is completed.

Bobolinks are a species of blackbird native to the grasslands of North and South America.

critical function of decomposition—processing the endless stream of dead organic material on the soil surface into nutrients usable to plants. But they also serve as food for the many species of insects and invertebrates that live in the soil with them. In one research study, as much as 300 to 650 pounds (136 to 295 kg) of these creatures were found to inhabit the top 6 inches (15 cm) of a plot of farmland soil.

Grassland insects are no slouches when it comes to sheer numbers either. One estimate claims that there may be as many as 1,000 insects in 1 square yard (0.91 m) of grassland. They eat more grasses and herbs than any other group of animals. Insects also help enrich the soil by aerating it and moving nutrients and organic material to lower layers, which helps feed the microscopic life in the soil. This in turn feeds the plants, which feed the grazing animals, which feeds the carnivores.

Worms not only eat grasses and aerate the soil, they are soil makers as well. Remnant bits of organic matter and minerals that they ingest are

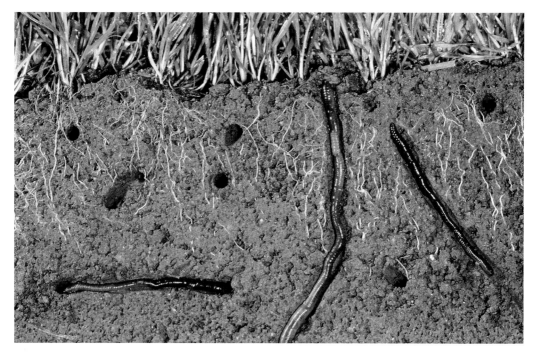

Worms are one of the most numerous creatures in the soil fauna, moving through and turning over tons of soil each year.

combined in their digestive system. They leave their droppings on the surface, and it adds to the soil layer. A few worms doing this might not seem like a big contribution, but when millions of them are doing it, 15 tons (13.6 metric tons) of soil can be added to every acre (0.4 hectares) of grassland each year. Over the course of fifty years, they can deposit 10 inches (25 cm) of topsoil on each acre (0.4 ha).

Hundreds of species of grasshoppers are common residents of grasslands around the world. Although most grasshoppers eat almost any plants, the lubber grasshopper of North American prairies does not eat grasses at all. Instead, it eat herbs, such as sunflowers. By eating these plants, these grasshoppers are unintentionally helping grasses to spread. It leaves more space for them to grow, and the grasses get more sunlight instead of being shaded by taller herbs.

LIVING WITH FIRE

The windy, hot climate of grasslands in the dry season, along with the lightweight, densely packed grasses and sudden lightning storms, provide the ideal recipe for wildfires. The gently rolling, open terrain allows fires to move quickly and efficiently, raging as fast as 40 miles per hour (64 kilometers per hour) and covering hundreds of square miles (hundreds of km²). No wonder Plains Indian tribes of North America referred to these fires as "red buffalo," comparing the fires to a stampede of the native buffalo herds.

Frequent fires are one of the reasons that trees and shrubs are uncommon in grasslands. There is little opportunity for the slower-growing, woody plants to set down roots and grow tall before a fire

Fires are common in grasslands. Most larger animals, like this hartebeest antelope, can outrun the flames.

sweeps through. By contrast, grasses often thrive after fires, since their growing points are at or below the ground, an area typically undamaged by the surface fires common in grasslands. Some researchers have said that without fires, grasses would be crowded out by shrubs and trees, and grasslands would eventually turn into forests.

However, in many grassland formations, some woody plant species have found ways to survive despite frequent fires. Pine trees have evolved fire-resistant bark, and the black wattle from Australia has seeds that only sprout after a fire has scorched the casings.

Most grassland plants store food reserves in underground root parts called tubers or rhizomes. Grasses also form growing points, which are like small buds on their roots, just below the soil surface. When the fire has passed through an area of savanna or prairie, they can quickly resprout, taking advantage of their stored reserves and the nutrients provided by ash from the fire, as well as the open space cleared by the fire. This new growth is rich in protein, so recently burned grasslands attract many more herbivores drawn to this highly nutritious food source.

Many grassland animals have evolved with fire, so they know how to escape its worst effects. Burrowing animals, such as prairie dogs, retreat into their underground tunnels, where the soil layers protect them from the heat of the fire. Some birds reap the benefits of fire's destructive effects, picking off insects, rodents, and lizards that are killed by or driven ahead of the fire. While large animals, like bison, elk, and deer, have the advantage of being able to outrun fires, sometimes fires move too fast even for them, and whole herds can be consumed by the raging infernos.

Seasonal fires are important to the ecological cycle of most grasslands and occur commonly during the dry seasons. Human-caused fires are common in these habitats as well. For native peoples everywhere, from Aborigines in Australia to Native Americans on North America's prairies, fire was an effective tool for removing trees and other shrubby vegetation in order to herd, to drive wild game for hunting, or even to

Tropical savannas, with their mix of vegetation, support many species of large animals, which feed not only on the grasses but also on the leaves of trees.

repel enemy invaders. Fire was also used by many cultures, ancient and modern, to clear land for farming. On the islands of the South Pacific, humans have been burning grasslands and other habitats to perpetuate and extend grassland habitat for centuries. And poachers on the Serengeti Plain often set fires intentionally to drive game animals from cover.

Many acres of natural grassland have been converted to cropland, such as this wheat field.

4

PEOPLE AND GRASSLANDS

Ever since humans first recognized grasslands as good hunting grounds, there has been a close relationship between people and this biome. Aside from the large herds of grazing animals, early peoples also soonrecognized that there were many edible plants growing on the savannas, prairies, and steppes. As humans evolved, they learned to cultivate grasses for food. Civilizations developed as farming became more successful, allowing large supplies of food to be grown and stored. Trade began, and cultures developed and intermingled.

FARMING

While grasses may not be the largest family of plants (although they are close), they are by far the most economically important. Many of the world's grasslands were converted to farms long ago, especially on those continents with a long history of human settlement, such as Africa and Europe. Today, many of these lands are still under cultivation, and new lands are being converted every day. As a result, natural grasslands are becoming more and more rare.

A vast majority of the crops that humans grow, fully 70 percent, are grass species—wheat, rice, barley, corn, millet, even sugar cane. The edible portion of most of these plants are the seeds, which are harvested and converted into other forms like flour and cereal before they are consumed or transformed into other products.

Corn, known as maize in many countries, is the largest cereal crop in the world. Grown largely in the United States and Canada, corn is used for animal feed, sweeteners such as corn syrup, and a fuel known as ethanol. For Mexicans, corn is a major food source.

Wheat is another important grass, and it is widely grown and harvested in China, India, and the United States. The flour made from wheat is the main ingredient in most of the world's breads. Russia is the largest grower of barley, another important cereal crop. Barley is used for animal feed, and a malted form is used in the production of beer and whiskey.

Rice is grown mainly in large shallow puddles, called paddies, in China, India, and Indonesia. The water helps to keep the weeds from invading the rice fields; it is drained off at harvest time. Many animals, such as herons, warblers, frogs, and snakes, use the flooded paddies as hunting grounds, eating a lot of insect pests that would otherwise damage the crops.

Like corn, sugar cane is a tall grass with thick stems, usually 7 to 20 feet (2 to 6 m) tall. Originally native to warmer regions of the world, sugar cane is now cultivated in many countries. Brazil, India, and China are the largest producers today. The sugar extracted from the sap is the main sweetener used around the world.

Tree-sized bamboos, the largest grasses in the world, are a major source of building materials in Asia. The wood's tough, lightweight quality makes it ideally suited for this and many other uses, including fences, furniture, musical instruments, and toys. Young, tender bamboo shoots are used for food, and the young stalks yield a sap used to make soft drinks and a sweet wine called Ulanzi. Other bamboo species are used to make baskets, hats, and roofing materials, among many other items.

Asian rice (Oryza sativa) *is the dominant species used for cultivation today and has been farmed for more than 6,500 years.*

Humans first learned to cultivate grasses as long as 10,000 years ago. Shortly thereafter, they started raising and keeping cattle, sheep, and goats, feeding them with the grasses they had raised.

This relatively reliable food source helped advance civilization, allowing cultures to develop and cities to thrive. Large parts of Europe have been converted over hundreds and thousands of years from forests and natural grasslands to agricultural fields and closely-cropped pastures. The British Isles were once largely forested, but gradually these forests were cut and the land converted to crop and livestock production to feed the growing human population. Today the rolling green fields of Britain are a much-loved, stereotypically English landscape, despite their man-made origins.

In some cases, grasslands are over-farmed. Continual planting year after year and excessive plowing and grazing can leave behind dry, nutrient-poor soils. This practice caused one of the greatest ecological disasters of the twentieth century, the Great Dust Bowl in the American Midwest. In the early 1930s, a long drought caused the overworked soil to loosen. Winds lifted the loose soils, forming "black blizzards" that blanketed parts of the country.

This farm field in Vermont was likely a floodplain forest before being converted to a farm field. Floodplain soils tend to be very rich in nutrients and are replenished during periodic floods.

LIVESTOCK AND GRAZING

Grasses were not only grown as food for humans; they were also grown as a ready supply of forage for domesticated animals, such as cattle, horses, sheep, goats, pigs, llamas, and others. In fact, humans were able to make livestock rearing much more efficient when they had learned to grow crops in a central location. Larger herds could be raised, and the drying and storage of grain allowed winter feeding of livestock, which kept the animals in good shape year-round.

Animals were raised for the meat they would bring once slaughtered, and they were also raised for the milk products (milk, cheese, butter, ice cream) and fiber and leather products (clothing, blankets, and leather belts, chaps, coats, shoes) that could be produced from them. Cultivation of grasses made all of this possible.

The large expanses of grasslands also enabled the rearing and feeding of livestock by pasturing. Pastures are fields of planted grasses and herbs used for cattle to range upon and feed at will. The larger rangelands allowed cattle to graze farther and wider. While this required less active management of the animals' food source, it did require shepherds or cattlemen to keep track of the flock or herd and move them between fields once grasses had been cropped close.

This intense pressure on the natural grasses of these rangelands has resulted, in many places, in a gradual change of grass species. In tallgrass and mixed-grass prairies of North America, the naturally occurring, taller grasses shade the soil, keeping it and the plant cover just above it relatively cool and moist. Constant grazing by livestock keeps these grasses closely cropped, allowing the sun and winds to dry out the soil. Over many years, this warmer, drier environment has encouraged more southerly species—which can tolerate these conditions—to invade.

Coastal California prairies have been so transformed by grazing and fire prevention that there are almost no native species in these ecosystems anymore. Species that are now growing in grasslands have been introduced, purposefully or accidentally, from other countries.

The California prairies have been grazed longer than any other North American grassland. Spanish settlers began ranching here in 1769. By the middle of the nineteenth century, after the California gold rush, the vast numbers of people flooding into the state caused a huge demand for beef. Cattle herds grew quickly to keep pace with the demand, and the grazing pressure on the landscape became more and more intense.

Grasslands today have evolved with the creatures who roamed and fed upon them. However, the numbers and concentrations of domesticated animals grazing this rich and essential biome have made the survival of many grassland residents—from prairie dogs and prairie gentians to red mites and nematodes—very uncertain indeed.

Burrowing owls live in the grasslands and deserts of North and South America. In the western United States, they raise their young in abandoned prairie dog burrows.

5

TEMPERATE GRASSLANDS

Temperate grasslands vary considerably between formations. The American prairies have very rich soils, while the Eurasian steppe soils can be nutrient-poor. These formations also experience weather extremes and are prone to fire. These variable conditions make temperate grasslands challenging places to live, but many creatures can and do live here, especially in the more fertile formations.

EURASIAN STEPPES

By far the largest expanse of temperate grassland in the world, the Eurasian steppe covers parts of many countries, from Russia through Turkmenistan, Kazakhstan, and Uzbekistan, into Afghanistan, Kyrgyzstan, Tajikistan, Mongolia, and China. The region ranges from 500 to 620 miles (800 to 1,000 km) wide to 5,000 miles (8,000 km) long. Because the Eurasian grassland formations extend over such a broad geographic area, there is a wide variety of steppe communities through-out Europe and Asia. These can be divided into a few general groups, based on the amount of rain they receive.

In general, steppes are shortgrass formations. Meadow steppe grows in moister climates and is mixed with trees and shrubs along riverbanks. Grasses here are the tallest of the steppe types, and the plants grow densely. True steppe is largely composed of bunchgrasses mixed with herbs in a semi-arid to arid (or dry) climate.

In desert steppe, grasses are short, spread out, and mixed with dwarf shrubs. Shrub-steppe features islands of shrubs amid the grasses and herbs. Alpine steppe can be found on spotty shallow soils in mountainous areas of China, such as on the Tibetan Plateau. Short grasses and cushion plants, low-growing plants arranged in tight clusters, are the common alpine steppe plants.

Steppe Wildlife

The most successful animals in the steppe formations are the rodents, most of which dig and live in burrows. Desert hamsters, Siberian chipmunks, ground squirrels, and marmots are common. Zokors are unique to the region and are related to blind mole rats. Like prairie dogs of the North American grasslands, the many species of steppe rodents are social and live in large groups.

Since the rodents are so plentiful, many carnivores have evolved to eat them. Weasels, polecats, foxes, and many birds of prey—goshawks, sparrowhawks, golden eagles, and black kites among them—keep the rodent populations in check. If the rodents were to become too numerous, they could overgraze the grasses, causing major changes to the ecology of the steppe.

However, the opposite has occurred in parts of the Eurasian steppe, such as in Mongolia. Many rodents have been poisoned because they are seen as pests by local farmers and ranchers. This poisoning not only reduces the predators' food source, it also poisons the meat-eaters as well.

Steppe eagles soar over the open grasslands of Asia and Africa, diving onto prey from above.

Many species of grazing animals historically roamed the steppe, including wild horses, stags, the Asiatic wild ass, and the saiga antelope. On the China steppe, the only grazing animals still around are the goitred gazelle and the Mongolian gazelle.

Grazers help maintain the balance of grasses and herbs in a healthy steppe ecosystem. With the disappearance of these animals, changes have occurred in plant species, and in some areas, herds of domesticated cattle have increased. With reduced grazing, grasses are replaced by herb species. With heavy, concentrated grazing—as with cattle—grasses take the place of herbs.

The Survival of the Saiga Antelope The saiga antelope is one of the most widespread grazing animals on the Eurasian steppe. Saiga historically traveled in herds of as many as 100,000 animals for protection, migrating great distances south in winter to search for food. This agile creature keeps an alert eye out for predators by jumping straight into the air to see over the tall grasses.

Saiga reproduce rather quickly. Females are able to mate at seven months old, and most of their births are twins. The males aid in their offsprings' survival by not eating during mating season. This leaves more food for the nursing mothers and their calves.

The fleshy nose of the saiga antelope helps to filter out dust in the dry summers and warms the cold winter air before it enters the animal's lungs.

Despite this efficient reproduction cycle, saiga antelope nearly became extinct in the early part of the twentieth century. The Soviet government worked with scientists to help the saiga's populations rebound. However, the saiga antelope is once again threatened. Illegal hunting, among other reasons, has caused a severe decline in the population of this symbol of the Eurasian steppe.

Numbering over 1 million individuals in the 1970s, the antelope population has been reduced to only about 50,000. While this may still seem like a large number, the makeup of the population is mostly female. Hunting pressure is heaviest on male saiga because their horns are prized by some Chinese people for their alleged medicinal properties. The few males that are left cannot mate with enough of the many female antelopes to keep the population growing. An international team of scientists and conservation groups is working with local governments to help stem the decline, but the future of the saiga antelope is far from certain.

NORTH AMERICAN PRAIRIES

The North American prairie covers the middle of the continent, from the Mackenzie River Delta in Canada to the central Mexican highlands. These grasslands once stretched for more than 914 million acres (370 million ha). Today, croplands have replaced much of the native grasslands, which now cover only about one-third of their original extent, at 309 million acres (125 million ha).

The native prairies can be divided into three major zones—tallgrass, mixed-grass, and shortgrass prairie. As with the Eurasian steppe, the difference in grass size is based largely on the amount of rain each zone receives. The immense Rocky Mountain range in the west forms a barrier to moist Pacific air traveling east, so the shortgrass prairie, lying right below the Rockies, receives little rain.

To the north and south, however, the way is clear for tropical air to blow north in summer and for frigid Arctic air to move south in winter. This creates varied and often violent weather conditions, with temperatures swinging wildly in short periods. Storms can arise suddenly, bringing high winds, lightning, tornadoes, and hail.

Despite these storms, the amount of rain that falls on the prairies is limited. The winter brings the driest and windiest weather, but the spring rains offer relief for a short time. Intense lightning storms light up the big open prairie skies in summer. During droughts, lightning can ignite the grasslands with quick-moving wildfires.

While grasses are the most prominent plants in North American prairies, only about three or four species grow in any given patch of grassland. A large amount of the plant cover consists of herbs and even dwarf shrubs.

Tallgrass Prairie

The easternmost zone, the tallgrass prairie, receives the most moisture in the form of rain and snow of all three zones. The rich soils were brought here by glaciers 12,000 years ago, and now dead grassland plants enrich them constantly. The moisture and soils allow taller species of grass, like big bluestem (named for the color of its young, bluish-green stems) and Indian grass, to dominate the plant cover. They can grow as tall as 8 feet (2.5 m).

Growing alongside the big bluestem are many species of grasses and herbs. Violets, orchids, and trout lilies make their appearance in spring, bringing the first burst of color to the monotonous winter greens and browns. Other wildflowers, like milkweed, indigo, and coneflowers keep the prairie brightly colored into the summer. Asters, goldenrod, and sunflowers bloom alongside the grasses in the height of summer. The grasses setting seed in the late summer and early autumn provide an ideal food source for migrating songbirds on their way south to warmer climates.

Prairie potholes are low areas of grassland where water collects. This region, also known as "North America's Duck Factory," covers millions of acres of grasslands in the Upper Midwest and provides habitat for more than half of the continent's waterfowl.

Along the eastern edge of its range, the tallgrass prairie mixes with the eastern deciduous forest to form a scattered band of grasses, trees, and shrubs. Unfortunately, most of the tallgrass prairie has been plowed under, and the land is now used to raise corn and soybeans and to serve as pasture for cattle.

Mixed-Grass Prairie

Mixed-grass prairie is a transition zone between the tall- and shortgrass prairies. The border between the mixed-grass prairie and the other two types is not easily defined; it shifts with changing climate and disturbance, natural or man-made, from grazing to fires.

Little bluestem, like many other mixed-grass prairie plants, can also be found in the other prairie types. Wheatgrasses and Canada wild rye

Sagebrush prairie grows in drier areas of the western United States. Although there are many different species of sagebrush, most are known for their strong odor, which is especially noticeable after rains.

(which grows along roadsides and in old fields) are also common in the mixed-grass prairie. Many of these grasses are intermediate in size, reaching 2 to 4 feet (0.6 to 1.2 m) tall. However, because this is a transition zone, it features the widest variety of plant sizes.

Large numbers of herbs and dwarf shrubs, such as sagebrush, sand-cherry, and low prairie rose, are also common in the mixed-grass prairie. Monarch butterflies can be seen throughout the summer drinking from common milkweed and showy milkweed, herb species that thrive here.

Shortgrass Prairie

Where grasslands butt up against the Rocky Mountains on the western extreme of their range lies the driest and shortest North American grassland, known as the shortgrass prairie. Because of the lack of moisture, the grasses are dormant and brown for nine months of the year, and they only reach a maximum height of about 1.5 feet (0.5 m).

Blue grama responds to light grazing by spreading in bunches. Once these bunches join, the grasses form mats. The shorter, hardy buffalo grass spreads its rhizomes through the soils to form mats. Many species of prairie wildlife feed on buffalo grass.

Prairie grasses have evolved strategies to deal with the dry conditions. They have many small, hairlike roots growing from each larger root that suck up any moisture in the soil. Shortgrass prairie plants also curl their leaves to hold in moisture.

The arid climate of shortgrass prairies even allows cacti to thrive. Prickly-pear cactus provides a showy spring display of large yellow or magenta flowers, while cholla (pronounced *choy-a*) and pincushion cactus show off their pink blossoms.

The Dust Bowl of the 1930s left the shortgrass prairie region as dry as a bone. Winds scattered the dry soils as far away as Europe, across the Atlantic Ocean. Most farmers abandoned their fields. Eventually, the grasslands came back on their own, although in a very different form than either before or after cultivation.

Other North American Grasslands

Several other patches of grassland exist that are particularly adapted to their unique climates and topography. They are separate and different enough from the other formations to merit their own descriptions.

Pacific prairie was once widespread between the Coast Range and the Sierra Nevada Mountains in California, as well as along the coast

The gopher snake is a common resident of the desert grassland of the southwestern United States. It is sometimes mistaken for a rattlesnake because it will coil itself, hiss, and rattle its tail when disturbed.

itself. Where the cities of Los Angeles and San Diego now sit was once a wide area of coastal grassland. This was a very rich region, with large herds of deer, elk, and pronghorn. Heavy grazing by domesticated cattle started in the Pacific prairie in the 1700s. Fire suppression by trained teams of federal and state firefighters intensified in the early 1900s. These teams aggressively fought both human-caused and natural fires (those caused by lightning). These and other actions helped change the natural communities of the Pacific prairie into grasslands made up of nonnative species that are inedible to most of the native wildlife.

A narrow strip of grasslands known as the coastal prairie stretches along the Gulf of Mexico coast from southwest Louisiana through Texas and into Mexico. Palouse prairie lies on the very dry and hilly

Columbian Plateau between the Cascade and Rocky Mountains in eastern Washington and Oregon. Desert grassland, the driest form, with widely scattered grasses, herbs, and shrubs, grows to the west of the short-grass prairies in the southwestern United States and northern Mexico.

Prairie Wildlife

As the North American prairie has changed with European settlement, so has the wildlife that calls the prairies home. Immense herds of large herbivores roamed the vast grassy expanses, including the American buffalo, pronghorn, bighorn sheep, elk, and deer. The huge numbers of these grazers brought in many thousands of carnivores that hunted them, such as gray wolves, mountain lions, and grizzly bears. More recently settled than any other comparable region in the world, the North American prairies provide a clear historical picture of the destruction of an ecosystem's native wildlife.

Standing 6 feet (1.8 m) tall at the shoulders, buffalo were the undisputed king of the prairies. It was estimated that 70 million buffalo roamed the prairies at the time that Francisco Vasques de Coronado, one of the first Europeans to see the continent, explored the southern prairie region from 1540 to 1542.

Many other species were adapted to the large buffalo herds and their effects on the landscape. Their trampling and grazing helped open up the dense grasslands, allowing a more diverse collection of native plants to germinate and grow. The openings they created were used by birds and lizards to hunt for insects. The buffalos' dead bodies nourished a host of different creatures, from beetles to vultures.

Only small herds of buffalo remain in farms and protected areas, such as Yellowstone National Park in Wyoming and Konza Prairie Biosphere Reserve in Kansas. Most were slaughtered by wide-eyed settlers in the nineteenth century who couldn't believe their luck at

The American buffalo or bison, the undisputed "king of the prairie," helped shape the North American grasslands. Only small herds still exist, such as these animals in South Dakota's Wind Cave National Park.

finding such a large supply of meat and hides ready for the taking. The many hunters, soldiers, and settlers traveling through the western United States during this period brought down the once-mighty herds. By the late nineteenth century, there were fewer than 1,000 wild buffalo roaming the North American grasslands. With their passing, the prairies changed. Many other species, such as foxes, vultures, eagles, and ravens, who became dependent on the habitat the larger creatures created, disappeared or moved to other areas.

The gray wolf was hunted down and killed with even more swiftness than the buffalo. This cunning and powerful predator was hated by many white settlers of the American prairies. Fearing for their own safety and the safety of their herds of sheep and cattle, settlers placed bounties on the wolves' heads, with the goal of ridding the country of them. Amazingly successful, this campaign resulted in the near extirpation — or local extinction — of the gray wolf in the lower forty-eight states.

With the wolf's passing, the coyote took its place. Smaller than the gray wolf, the coyote preyed on smaller species, drastically reducing the populations of swift foxes and ground-nesting birds. Because the wolf wasn't around to hunt larger animals, there were fewer of their carcasses around for scavengers to feed upon.

Pronghorn have survived in greater numbers than the buffalo. Probably 1 million of these swift prairie animals remain out of a historical estimate in the tens of millions. Related to both antelopes and goats,

Impressive speed, stamina and agility, as well as excellent eyesight, help the pronghorn avoid predators on the North American prairies.

pronghorn prefer the shortgrass prairie, munching on herbs and shrubs, keeping an especially acute eye out for predators. While not a true antelope, pronghorn are as fast as their relatives; indeed, they are the fastest North American mammal. Their long legs and double-size heart allow pronghorn to travel for miles at speeds of 45 mph (72 kph), with bursts up to 60 mph (97 kph), if needed, to elude predators.

Many animals still survive and some even flourish in today's prairies. Prairie dogs, deer mice, and ground squirrels feed on the many species of grasses and herbs, both above- and belowground parts. In turn, these rodents become food for the smaller prairie predators—ferrets, badgers, swift and red foxes, hawks, and eagles.

Prairie dog towns can occupy large areas, and provide habitat for many other species of plants and animals.

Dog Towns

Five species of prairie dogs populate the prairies of North America. These members of the squirrel family have a very tight-knit social structure, with each clan, or family unit, fiercely guarding their territory, even passing it down from generation to generation.

Prairie dogs are what ecologists call a keystone species because they fill a necessary role in shortgrass prairie ecosystems. Without their burrowing to provide the right soil conditions for grasses and herbs to develop, the shortgrass prairie wouldn't exist in its current state. Many other animals wouldn't flourish here either. Some species depend directly on prairie dog burrows. Burrowing owls raise their young in abandoned burrows. Eastern cottontail rabbits and western rattlesnakes also live in them.

Other animals rely on the scattered plant cover to hunt, hide, and nest. Birds hunt insects that frequent prairie dog towns. Rattlesnakes, hawks, foxes, coyotes, badgers, bobcats, and other predators hunt prairie dogs and other prey.

In the early twentieth century, one Texas prairie dog town was estimated to contain about 400 million animals and covered 25,000 square miles (65,000 km^2). Less than 1 percent of the black-tailed prairie dog's North American habitat is currently occupied. Disease, change in habitat from grassland to agricultural fields and housing developments, and poisoning and shooting have decimated their populations. Ranchers fear the damage the prairie dog towns do to their cattle ranges, so they exterminate them.

The maned wolf is well adapted to its grassland habitat in the South American cerrado. Their large ears allow them to hear rodents moving in dense vegetation, and their long legs provide them the height to see over the tall grasses and shrubs.

TROPICAL SAVANNAS

Savannas occur throughout the tropical regions of the world. From the savannas of Africa and Australia and the monsoonal grasslands of Asia, to the llanos, *cerrado*, and *campos* of South America, each formation is unique.

Because these grassland formations often include shrubs and trees as well as grasses and herbs, we can identify many types of savannas. These types include tree savanna, woodland savanna, shrub savanna, and grass savanna. Tree savannas are further divided according to the major tree type: acacia savanna, palm savanna, and pine savanna, for example.

Like temperate grasslands, there are similar animal species common to each savanna formation. However, savannas are unusual in that entirely different animal groups fill the same niche—or perform the same ecological function—in each formation. Hoofed animals are only common grazers on the African savanna. Large birds take their place in South American formations, while kangaroos are the major grass-eaters in Australian savannas.

THE SERENGETI PLAIN

Imagine flying low over thousands of square miles of rolling grassy plain. Lush green grasses surround large pools of standing water. The pools are fringed with hundreds and sometimes thousands of animals — wildebeests, zebras, lions, elephants, rhinoceroses, warthogs, ostriches, and many, many more. This is what the German naturalist Bernhard Grzimek saw fifty years ago, when he conducted the first-ever research on the ecology and wildlife of Africa's Serengeti Plain.

The Serengeti Plain is the largest and most widely known savanna formation on Earth. Many books have been written and documentaries made about this unbelievably rich ecosystem. Much of today's knowledge of the ecology of the Serengeti is the result of years of research by Grzimek.

Africa's Serengeti Plain is a patchwork of woodland and savanna.

Animals on the Move

The savannas of the Serengeti Plain draw the largest diversity and greatest numbers of wild grazing animals in the world. Many species of antelope—impalas, gazelles, eland, kudu, oryx, and gerenuk—as well as wildebeests, elephants, giraffes, hippopotamuses, Cape buffalo, and zebras graze on the savannas, sometimes together in mixed herds.

Each species has its own particular food, time of day, and season to feed in a specific part of the Serengeti. Grzimek determined this by flying over the vast stretches of savanna with his son, Michael, in their zebra-striped plane, landing at each change of grass type and sampling the plants and soils they found there. For example, red oat grass and Rhodes grass are common in the drier regions of the Serengeti. Grzimek was able to tie the grassland type to different grazing species of animals.

Through this link, he showed how each herd migrated—or traveled from one region to another—when their food source became scarce or when the dry season forced the plants to go dormant. He followed the herds on their treks, to the shortgrass plains of the southeastern Serengeti after the November rains began, and then back to the western tallgrass-acacia savanna in June, after the rains ceased and the shortgrass plains dried. The animals covered up to 50 miles (80 km) a day and traveled as far as 1,000 miles (1,600 km) round-trip from one feeding ground to another.

With so many large herds of grazers roaming the open plains, predators like lions, cheetahs, leopards, wild dogs, jackals, and hyenas are also plentiful on the Serengeti. They roam around the herds, waiting for an opportunity to pounce. The big cats will prey upon any animal, while hyenas usually only attack the young, weak, or old.

The herding behavior of grazing animals may have evolved for protection. This large mass of bodies can provide an effective barrier, especially when they are stampeding. As the old saying goes, there is safety in numbers.

Varied Wildlife

Other animal groups are also highly diverse on the Serengeti. Savanna habitat, with its wide open fields full of small creatures to hunt and scattered trees for perching and nesting, seems to have been made-to-order for birds of prey. More than sixty species of hawks, eagles, and vultures and twelve species of owl hunt the many rodents and other small savanna animals. One of the most unusual raptors is the tall, storklike, elegantly plumed secretary bird, which roams the grasslands, crushing snakes and rousting mice with its large feet.

Reptiles are also well represented on the Serengeti Plain. Freshwater crocodiles—which can be 1,000 pounds (454 kg) and 18 feet (5.5 m) long—inhabit the rivers, feasting upon animals as large as wildebeests.

Although it does fly and roosts in trees, the secretary bird—also known as "Africa's marching eagle"—spends most of its time on the ground in savannas, covering 12 to 19 miles (20 to 30 km) a day searching for food.

Like miniature mountains, termite mounds dot the landscape of the Serengeti. These cheetahs are using the mounds for shade and perhaps as cover from their prey.

Snakes include the boomslang, the black mamba, and the rock python, which can kill and eat small gazelles. Many species of lizard, including the flap-necked chameleon and the rainbow skink, are common. The beautifully patterned leopard tortoise can reach 30 inches (76 cm) in length and feeds mainly on grasses and herbs.

Another common sight in many savannas are tall earthen mounds, seemingly shaped by a human hand. Surprisingly, though, they are the work of insects, namely termites. These mounds serve as the home bases for their colonies. In some savannas, in areas where the soil between mounds is too thin or wet, the mounds also provide places for trees to take root.

Termites and ants have been a part of the savanna ecosystem for so long that predators have evolved specifically to hunt them. Aardvarks have strong claws for digging into mounds and long snouts for rooting out the insects in their earthen homes. The aardwolves (unrelated to aardvarks) are another termite predator, but this one is part of the cat family and looks more like a small hyena. Both creatures are nocturnal, meaning they are active only at night.

Protecting the Serengeti

Many wild animals on the Serengeti Plain are hunted illegally, sometimes to the point of extinction. In fact, once the Kenya-Uganda railroad opened up this formerly untouched region to travel and trade in the early 1900s, huge numbers of wild animals were slaughtered, most notably by soldiers during the two world wars.

Fortunately, people have long recognized the spectacular importance of this rich region. Some countries have set aside portions of the savanna and adjacent forests in reserves, conservation areas, and parks, such as Tanzania's 5,000-square-mile (12,950- km²) Serengeti National Park.

Bernhard Grzimek was a tireless advocate for the animals of the Serengeti and worked with the Tanzanian government to set aside land for the park. These and other actions have helped to stem the slaughter and allow more than 1.5 million animals to continue to roam the all-embracing grassy plains.

LLANOS

South America contains a great deal of the world's savanna formations. The llanos cover 174,000 square miles (450,000 km²), while Brazil's cerrado is even larger, covering 790,000 square miles (2 million km²).

Each year, between April and November, the rainy season brings floods to the Orinoco River basin in northern South America. The river snakes its way through the countries of Venezuela and Colombia,

The annual flooding of the llanos nourishes the plant life of these floodplain grasslands.

carrying its load of silt and sand washed down from the Guiana Highlands and the Andes Mountains out into the Atlantic Ocean. After the rains end and the river recedes, much of this soil settles out along the floodplain, nourishing the savanna region called Llanos del Orinoco. The annual flooding not only provides nutrients to the grasses that grow here, it also keeps trees from taking root in the shifting soil.

The lowlands of the Llanos del Orinoco are concentrated around the many rivers that feed the Orinoco River basin. As a result, many lowland llanos animals are aquatic or at least use the river waters for some purpose.

The capybara, an enormous rodent that thrives in the grassy margins of the Orinoco feeding on the grasses and herbs, is not aquatic, but readily plunges into the water when danger draws close. These large rodents, 4 feet (1.2 m) long and weighing up to 100 pounds (45 kg), are a tasty meal for the many cougars, jaguars, and even boa constrictors that live along or frequent the floodplain area.

The Orinoco, or Arrau, turtle is, at 110 pounds (50 kg), the largest river turtle in the Americas. Females can reach 2 feet (0.61 m) long. They nest in riverbanks during the dry season and feed on fruits and seeds of trees. This turtle is widely eaten by native peoples, and it is considered a delicacy by rich city dwellers. Turtle nests are robbed of eggs and soup is made from their meat. As a result, the Orinoco turtle, as well as other turtles in the region, are faced with extinction.

The largest rodent in the world, the capybara feasts on the rich vegetation of the llanos, moving between the exposed river shoals in the dry season and the grassy banks during floods.

About the size of a large dog, giant anteaters are docile creatures that can eat as many as 30,000 ants or termites in a single day.

Like other savanna formations, llanos are rich in ants and termites and, as in Africa, animals have evolved specifically to prey on them. The giant anteater, ecologically equivalent but unrelated to aardvarks and aardwolves of the Serengeti, has a long snout and tongue. It tears apart anthills and termite mounds with its sharp claws, feasting on the tiny treats with its long snout.

The armadillo, an unusual mammal with hard-shelled body plates, also feeds on termites. To protect itself against predators, the armadillo digs into the ground with its sharp claws. The creature lies in the hole with its belly to the ground and only its plate-covered back exposed, making it difficult for any predator to attack.

CERRADO

Stretching atop the Brazilian highlands and covering over 20 percent—about 770,000 square miles (2,000,000 km²)—of the immense state of Brazil, the cerrado is a biological jewel in a continent with a full crown.

While not numerous, jaguarundis are widespread in Central and South America. They prefer habitats with dense vegetation to hunt in, so cerrados are perfect for them.

The cerrado is made up of many different types of savanna. *Campo limpo* are treeless expanses of grasses and herbs, much like prairies in appearance. *Campo sujo* are shrubby grasslands, while *campo cerrado* are mixed woodland and grassland that remain somewhat open, with large spaces between trees. Yet another type, *cerradão,* contains the most trees and is more closed and shady than the other types. It is often a transition type between forest and grassland. Many cerradão trees have thick bark, leathery leaves, and deep roots, all adaptations to fire, an important, natural part of this savanna formation.

This highly diverse ecosystem supports many endemic species. Nearly half of the cerrado's 10,000 species of herbs and grasses grow only in this region. Many bird species make use of the cerrado, including the rhea, a large flightless bird related to the ostrich. The golden-red maned wolf hunts the cerrado, feasting on the many rodents and small mammals. The ocelot, the jaguar, and the jaguarundi also favor the semi-open grasslands.

Like other tropical formations, the cerrado is alive with reptiles and amphibians, including many snakes, tree frogs, and the giant worm lizard. Insects have not been well studied, but estimates of their numbers and diversity are also high.

Human development in the cerrado region was limited until very recently. Roughly two hundred different native groups live in or make use of the cerrado, but their impact is limited. The Brazilian government built a new capital city, Brasilia, in the heart of the cerrado in the mid-twentieth century. Since then, many farms have been established, allowing Brazil to supply much of its own grain supply, namely soy and corn. Millions of cattle now also roam the region.

All of these changes are bringing devastating effects to the natural diversity of the cerrado. Only about 20 percent of the native vegetation remains, and only 5 percent of the Brazilian cerrado is protected in reserves or parks.

Big Birds

One group of birds has a representative in each of the major savanna formations. These birds, known by their scientific name as ratites, are all large and flightless. They have long necks, plump bodies, and long legs—all good adaptations for seeing over tall grasses and running quickly across the open ground to escape predators. The males of all three species sit on the nests, incubating the eggs.

African savannas are the home of the ostrich, the most well-known of this group. Their long, thinly feathered necks and their round, plump, brown-feathered bodies atop tall, thin legs are almost comical in appearance. The tallest and heaviest bird in the world at 8 feet (2.5 m) and up to 330 pounds (150 kg), their heads rise over the backs of the wildebeests and zebras they often travel with. Their sharp vision and excellent hearing can detect danger quickly. The ostriches are an advantage to the herds, alerting them to predators.

Ostriches are well suited to an ecosystem prone to drought. They do not need to drink because they get all their moisture from the plants they eat. These birds don't have the complex stomachs that hoofed mammals do, so they regularly eat sand and small stones, which helps them to break down and digest plant material.

Emus are the Australian equivalent of ostriches. Not quite as tall, at 5 to 6 feet (1.6 to 1.9 m), emus have a thick, shaggy, grayish-brown feather coat. Their heads have black feathers surrounding a blue-skinned face. They have very distinctive calls—females make a booming or drumming sound, while males voices are harsher.

This ratite feeds on fruits, seeds, insects, and small animals. Emus can run nearly 40 mph (60 kph) across the Australian grasslands, making a zigzag pattern to avoid predators. While they do occur in a wide range of habitats, they prefer both savanna and mediterranean scrub forest.

This ability to take advantage of multiple habitats has allowed the emu to expand its range, despite increasing human development. Highly adaptable, emus will stay in one location if the habitat is good. However, when drought occurs, they will travel hundreds of miles to find food and water.

The least known of the ratites may be the rhea, from the South American pampas and savannas. Two species of rhea occupy these grasslands, although the smaller of the two, Darwin's rhea, also can be found well up into the Andes Mountains. The larger species, known as the greater rhea, is smaller than both the ostrich and the emu but still stands tall at 5 feet (1.6 m). Their wings are longer in relation to their body size than the other ratites' wings. Rheas appear to use them to gain speed and to hold themselves stable when turning quickly.

A greater rhea.

CONCLUSION

CONSERVING GRASSLANDS

Despite the fact that the grassland biome is one of the largest on Earth, natural grasslands are becoming more and more rare. Because of the flat landscape, their rich soils, the usefulness of grassland plants, the ease with which these plants are cultivated, and the mixing of grassland species worldwide, many native grasslands have been transformed into agricultural croplands, pastures for livestock, and housing developments. Most of these converted and managed grasslands, are made up mostly of nonnative plants and animals. The native species and connections between them, which are so important to natural grasslands, are being lost at an alarming rate.

While many grassland areas have already been settled by humans and used for agriculture and pasture for thousands of years, there are currently many other regions actively being put under plow and hoof, such as the Brazilian cerrado, one of the most biologically diverse savanna formations on the planet.

Other than their utility as agricultural lands, grasslands are often lost because there is too little attention paid to their plight. More often, it is forests of different kinds, such as tropical rainforests, old-growth forests, and boreal forests, that receive the most attention by the conservation

Grasslands are often maintained for and by domesticated animals, such as these llamas. Llamas are raised today for their wool and were formerly used as pack animals by the ancient Incas.

community and the public. While these are all worthy of saving, the grasslands are often neglected as a focus for conservation.

However, many grasslands are as rich or richer in diversity than some forests. The North American prairies play host to more than three-quarters of the country's bird species. Many insect species rely on grassland plants for food and breeding, while the plants that they polli-nate rely on them for survival. If any of the plants or the pollinators are lost, a link in the chain of grassland ecology is broken, and the system is damaged.

A damaged grassland, such as steppe or prairie, may take decades or longer to recover from disturbance, if it ever does recover. More often, grasslands need help, and some conservation groups are focusing on this. Scientists are rapidly trying to catalog species of grassland plants and animals before many of these areas disappear or are damaged beyond repair. More attention needs to be paid to them, for grassland regions are not merely good locations for farms or houses, but good locations for grasslands. Let's try to keep them that way.

Research on the grasslands of the Elizabeth Islands off the coast of Massachusetts is being conducted to determine how best to control invasions by nonnative, invasive plants.

GLOSSARY

adaptation—A change in behavior or structure that allows an organism, such as a bird or a grass, to survive or even improve its condition in relation to a changing environment; the deep roots of big bluestem grass are an adaptation to an environment prone to frequent droughts.

cereal—A grass plant, such as corn, barley, wheat, or rice; or, the grains harvested from these grasses and used as food.

cultivate—To plow and till land in order to grow crops.

decomposition—The natural breakdown or decay of organic material; often carried out by bacteria, molds, soil invertebrates, and insects.

dormancy—A period of rest or inactivity during a time of stress, such as in a cold or dry season; some grassland plants go dormant to avoid drought.

ecologist—A scientist who studies ecological systems; this includes not only species of organisms but also the connections between these species and their environments.

evolution—The process of adaptation by an organism, over generations, to a changing environment; this usually results in a new species, one which cannot mate with its former kin.

fertilization—The beginning stage of biological reproduction, involving the joining of a male reproductive cell with a female reproductive cell to form a new cell that develops into a new individual.

floodplain—A plain or other flat area next to the lower reaches of a river; these areas are subject to periodic flooding and often contain species of plants that are adapted to the flooded conditions.

germination—The sprouting of a seed.

groundwater—An underground reservoir of water that supplies springs, rivers, streams, lakes, and wells. This water does not usually exist as underground pools, but within cracks between rocks and as saturated soil.

humus—The top layers of soil in a grassland or other heavily vegetated ecosystem, made up of partially and fully decomposed plant material. This layer provides plants with essential nutrients and holds water close to the soil surface, easier for plants to use.

latitude—A measure of distance—described in degrees, minutes, and seconds—on Earth's surface north and south of the equator. On a map or globe, these are the horizontal lines circling Earth.

migration—A periodic movement of an individual or a group of animals from one location to another in response to food availability.

niche—A role or function filled by an organism in an ecosystem; buffalo occupied a niche as the primary grazing animal on the North American prairies, while kangaroos occupy this niche in Australian grasslands.

pollen—The collection of microscopic spores or grains produced by the anthers (male parts) of a flowering plant.

pollination—The transfer of pollen from a male flower to a female flower; this initiates the reproductive process in plants.

pollinator—An animal agent of pollination, such as a bee, fly, bird, or bat.

FIND OUT MORE

Books

Johansson, Philip. *The Wide Open Grasslands: A Web of Life,* Berkeley Heights, NJ: Enslow Publishers, 2004.

Toupin, Laurie Peach. *Life in the Temperate Grasslands.* New York: Franklin Watts, 2005.

Wallace, Marianne D. *America's Prairies and Grasslands: Guide to Plants and Animals.* Golden, CO: Fulcrum Resources, 2001.

Web Sites

http://www.blueplanetbiomes.org
This site provides basic information about biomes.

http://mbgnet.mobot.org
Designed specifically for kids, this Missouri Botanical Garden Web site describes biomes and ecosystems in a simple, straightforward way.

http://www.nceas.ucsb.edu/nceas-web/kids/biomes/biomes_home.htm
The Kids Do Ecology page of the National Center for Ecological Analysis and Synthesis has concise information on the world's biomes and links to other Web sites.

BIBLIOGRAPHY

Australian Museum Online. "Bird Fact Sheets: Emu *(Dromaius novaehollandiae)*."
  http://www.austmus.gov.au/
Conservation International. "Biodiversity Hotspots: Cerrado."
  http://www.biodiversityhotspots.org
Jones, Stephen R., and Ruth Carol Cushman. 2004. *A Field Guide to the North American
  Prairie.* Boston: Houghton Mifflin Company. Konza Prairie Biological Station, Kansas
  State University. http://www.k-state.edu/konza
LaBelle, Jason M. "Late Pleistocene and Early Holocene Hunter-Gatherers of the Pampas
  and Patagonia, Argentina and Chile." May 20, 2002. http://www.ele.net
May, Holly L. "Black-Tailed Prairie Dog *(Cynomys ludovicianus)*" Fish and Wildlife Habitat
  Management Leaflet Number 23, July 2001.
Wildlife Habitat Council and Wildlife Habitat Management Unit, Natural Resources
  Conservation Service. http://wildlife.state.co.us/species_cons/PrairieDog
  NRCS_Bulletin.pdf
Neotropical Grassland Conservancy. http://www.conservegrassland.org
Ojasti, Juhani. "Wildlife Utilization in Latin America: Current Situations and Prospects for
  Sustainable Management (FAO Conservation Guide - 25)." 1996. Food and
  Agriculture Organization of the United Nations, Corporate Document Repository.
  http://www.fao.org/documents
Pyne, Stephen J., Patricia L. Andrews, and Richard D. Laven. 1996. *Introduction to Wildland
  Fire, Second Edition.* New York: John Wiley & Sons, Inc.
Roach, John. "Rare Antelope on the Brink of Extinction, Scientists Say," National
  Geographic News, April 25, 2003. Cited in: Biodiversity Conservation Center,
  http://www.biodiversity.ru/eng/;
  http://www.saigak.biodiversity.ru/eng/publications/ngn250403.html
Stein, Sara. 1993. *Noah's Garden.* Boston: Houghton Mifflin Company.
United Nations Educational, Scientific, and Cultural Organization. Konza Prairie, Biosphere
  Reserve Information, UNESCO–MAB Biospheres Reserve Directory.
  http://www2.unesco.org/mab/br/brdir/directory/biores.asp?code=USA+28&mode=all
The Venezuela Ecoportal. "Venezuela's Eco-Regions: Llanos." http://ecoalliance.tripod.com
Wildwatch: African Wildlife and Conservation. "Birds: Ostrich—Longest Legs, Largest
  Eyes." http://www.wildwatch.com

INDEX

Tom Warhol is a photographer, writer, and naturalist from Massachusetts, where he lives with his wife, their dog, and two cats. Tom holds both a BFA in photography and an MS in forest ecology. Tom has worked for conservation groups such as The Nature Conservancy, managing nature preserves, and The American Chestnut Foundation, helping to grow blight-resistant American chestnut trees. He currently works for the Massachusetts Riverways Program, helping to care for sick, injured, and resident hawks, eagles, and owls. In addition to the Earth's Biomes series, Tom has authored books for Marshall Cavendish Benchmark's AnimalWays series, including *Hawks* and *Eagles.* He also writes for newspapers such as the *Boston Globe.* His landscape, nature, and wildlife photographs can be seen in exhibitions, in publications, and on his Web site, www.tomwarhol.com.